T0191238

EXCELLENCE

JOEL OSTEEN

NEW YORK • NASHVILLE

Also by Joel Osteen

15 Ways to Live Longer and Healthier
15 Ways to Live Longer and Healthier Study Guide

All Things Are Working for Your Good
Daily Readings from All Things Are Working for Your Good

Blessed in the Darkness
Blessed in the Darkness Journal
Blessed in the Darkness Study Guide

Break Out!
Break Out! Journal
Daily Readings from Break Out!

Digest Books
Believe
Stay in the Game
The Abundance Mind-set
Two Words That Will Change Your Life Today

Empty Out the Negative
A Fresh New Day Journal

Every Day a Friday
Every Day a Friday Journal
Daily Readings from Every Day a Friday

Fresh Start
Fresh Start Study Guide

I Declare
I Declare Personal Application Guide

Next Level Thinking
Next Level Thinking Journal
Next Level Thinking Study Guide
Daily Readings from Next Level Thinking

Peaceful on Purpose
Peaceful on Purpose Study Guide
Peace for the Season

Psalms and Proverbs for Everyday Life

Speak the Blessing

Rule Your Day
Rule Your Day Journal

The Power of Favor
The Power of Favor Study Guide

The Power of I Am
The Power of I Am Journal
The Power of I Am Study Guide
Daily Readings from The Power of I Am

Think Better, Live Better
Think Better, Live Better Journal
Think Better, Live Better Study Guide
Daily Readings from Think Better, Live Better

With Victoria Osteen
Our Best Life Together
Wake Up to Hope Devotional

You Are Stronger than You Think
You Are Stronger than You Think Study Guide

You Can, You Will
You Can, You Will Journal
Daily Readings from You Can, You Will

Your Best Life Now
Your Best Life Begins Each Morning
Your Best Life Now for Moms
Your Best Life Now Journal
Your Best Life Now Study Guide
Daily Readings from Your Best Life Now
Scriptures and Meditations for Your Best Life Now
Starting Your Best Life Now

Your Greater Is Coming
Your Greater Is Coming Study Guide

EXCELLENCE

FaithWords
Hachette Book Group
1290 Avenue of the Americas, New York, NY 10104
faithwords.com
X.com/faithwords

First Edition: June 2024

FaithWords is a division of Hachette Book Group, Inc. The FaithWords name and logo are registered trademarks of Hachette Book Group, Inc.

The publisher is not responsible for websites (or their content) that are not owned by the publisher.

The Hachette Speakers Bureau provides a wide range of authors for speaking events. To find out more, go to hachettespeakersbureau.com or email HachetteSpeakers@hbgusa.com.

Literary development: Lance Wubbels Literary Services, Bloomington, Minnesota.

Library of Congress Cataloging-in-Publication Data

Names: Osteen, Joel, author.
Title: Excellence / Joel Osteen.
Description: First edition. | New York : FaithWords, Hachette Book Group, 2024.
Identifiers: LCCN 2023051862 | ISBN 9781546007562 (hardcover) | ISBN 9781546007579 (ebook)
Subjects: LCSH: Excellence—Religious aspects—Christianity. | Christian life.
Classification: LCC BV4509.5 .O869 2024 | DDC 248.4—dc23/eng/20240424
LC record available at https://lccn.loc.gov/2023051862

ISBN: 9781546007562 (hardcover), 9781546007579 (ebook)

Printed in the United States of America

LSC

Printing 2, 2024

Contents

1. Commit to Excellence   1
2. Don't Settle for Good Enough   23
3. Keep Growing   43
4. Stay Focused   67
5. Stay Passionate   91

1

Commit to Excellence

For many people, mediocrity is the norm; they want to do as little as they possibly can and still get by. But God did not create us to be mediocre or average. He doesn't want us to just barely get by or to do what everybody else is doing. God has called us to be a cut above. He's called us to stand out in the crowd, to be people of excellence and integrity. Indeed, the only way to be truly happy is to live with excellence and integrity.

What does it mean to be a person of excellence? When you have a spirit of excellence, you do your best whether anyone is watching or not.

You go the extra mile. You do more than you have to. Other people may complain about their jobs. They may go around looking sloppy and cutting corners. Don't sink to that level. Everyone else may be slacking off at work, compromising in school, letting their lawns go, but here's the key: You are not everyone else. You take pride in your work and in who you are. God wants you to set the highest standard.

You should be the model employee for your company. Your boss and your supervisors should be able to say to the new hires, "Watch him. Learn from her. Pick up the same habits. Develop the same skills. This person is the cream of the crop, always on time, has a great attitude, and does more than what is required."

When you have an excellent spirit like that, you will not only see promotion and increase but you are honoring God. Some people think, *Let me go to church to honor God. Let me read my Bible to honor God.* And, yes, that's true, but it honors God just as much to get to work on time.

It honors God to be productive. It honors God to look good each day.

When you are excellent, your life gives praise to God. That's one of the best witnesses you can have. Some people will never go to church. They never listen to a sermon. They're not reading the Bible. Instead, they're reading your life. They're watching how you live. Now don't be sloppy. When you leave the house, whether you're wearing shorts or a three-piece suit, make sure you look the best you possibly can. When you go to work, don't slack off and don't give a half-hearted effort. Give it your all. Do your job to the best of your ability. You're representing Almighty God. You should be so full of excellence that other people want what you have.

Exceed Expectations

When you're a person of excellence, you do more than necessary. It's interesting that Jesus told His disciples, "If a soldier demands you carry his gear one mile, carry it two miles." At that time, Roman soldiers were permitted by law to require someone else to carry their armor. He was saying, "Don't just meet the minimum requirements. Do more than is expected. Go the extra mile." That's the attitude you need to have: *I'm not doing just what I have to. I'm not doing the minimum amount to keep my job. I'm a person of excellence. I go above and beyond what's asked of me. I do more than is expected.*

This means if you're supposed to be at work at 8:00 a.m., you show up ten minutes early. You produce more than you have to. You stay ten minutes late. You don't start shutting down thirty minutes before closing. You put in a full day. Many people show up to work fifteen minutes late. They get some coffee, wander around the office, and finally sit down to work a half hour late. They'll waste another half hour making personal phone calls and surfing the Internet. That's especially tempting for people who are working from home where no one is watching. Then they wonder why they aren't promoted. It's because God doesn't reward sloppiness. God rewards excellence.

In the Old Testament, Abraham sent his servant to a foreign country to find a wife for his son, Isaac. Abraham told the servant that God would send an angel before him to help. When the servant reached the city of Abraham's brother, Nahor, around sunset, the women were coming out to draw water from the well. He prayed that he would know that he'd found the right lady if she offered a drink to both him and his camels. When a beautiful young lady named Rebekah came to the well, the servant said, "I'm so thirsty. Would you mind lowering your bucket and getting me a drink?" She said, "Not only that, let me draw water for your camels as well."

Here's what's interesting. After a long day's walk, a camel can drink thirty gallons of water. This servant had ten camels with him. Think about what Rebekah did. If she had a one-gallon bucket, she said, in effect, "Yes, I'll not only do what you asked and give you a drink, but I'll also dip down in this well three hundred more times and give your ten camels a drink."

Rebekah went way beyond the call of duty. As a result, she was chosen to marry Isaac, who came from Abraham's wealthy family. I doubt that she ever again had to draw three hundred gallons of water. God rewards excellence. When you do more than what's required, you will see God's goodness in new ways.

You may be declaring favor and promotion over your life, and that's all good, but it's only one part. The second part is making sure you get to work on time, do more than what's required, and do better this year than last year. We're in a very competitive marketplace. If you're not growing, improving, and learning new skills, you're falling behind.

On Sunday afternoons after our final service, I sit down with a video editor and I edit my own sermons. I've done over 900 messages over the years. You might think that I don't need to watch another one, that if I haven't gotten my delivery down by now, it's never going to happen. Still, I study each one to see what's good and what could be better. I'll see that one point took a little too long to develop or that another section of the message was really great. Maybe I'll see that I'm talking a little fast or that I need to look out at one side of the audience more. I'm constantly evaluating and analyzing not only my speaking performance, but also the production, the lighting, and the camera angles. My attitude is that there's always room for improvement. We can always get better.

People who watch our services on television will sometimes say, "Joel, I never hear you stutter, and I never hear you make a mistake." I always tell them it's because I know how to edit. I did that for seventeen years before I became the pastor. I can fix every stutter, every pause. I don't have to. My live broadcasts aren't bad, but I want my taped sermons to be the best they can possibly be. I don't want to be at the same level next year as I am now. I want to be more effective, more skilled, and making a greater impact.

Strive for Excellence

When you're an excellent person, you don't get stagnant. You're always taking steps to improve. Favor and being excellent go hand in hand. Increase, promotion, and reaching your highest potential are all tied to a spirit of excellence. Looking your best and taking care of your possessions are also part of this lifestyle. Some people, and I say this respectfully, drive cars that look as though they've never been washed. It used to be two-tone. Now it's four-tone. It would get better gas mileage if they washed it. They argue that it's an old piece of junk and that they're planning on getting a better car. But if you don't take care of what God has given you, how can He bless you with more?

I've been in huts in Africa with dirt floors and no running water, but they were spotless. Everything was clean, organized, perfectly in place. Why is that? The people who live there have a spirit of excellence. Whether you have much or a little, whether it's old or new, take pride in what God has given you.

After services in our church, I usually walk up to the visitor area to greet our guests. On the way, if I see a piece of paper on the floor, a gum wrapper or a bulletin, I pick it up. I don't have to do that. Somebody on our staff will get it eventually, but when you have this spirit of excellence, it's ingrained in you. To see any trash on the floor rubs me the wrong way. Sometimes children from our nurseries drop crackers on the hallway floor. I always ask my assistant to call the cleaning crew if there is a big mess. I don't want people coming to the next service to see that on the floor. Why is that? It's not excellence if there is a mess on the floor. I realize our building represents Almighty God. I have a responsibility to make sure it looks excellent. That's why we keep it painted. We make sure the lawn looks perfect, the hallways are spotless, the equipment works, the cameras are state-of-the-art, and the broadcast is exceptional.

Why? We represent God, and He is not

sloppy. God is not run-down. God is not second-class. He is an excellent God. It doesn't mean you have to have the best to represent Him, but you should take care of what you have as best you can. Sometimes a can of paint can make all the difference in the world. Pulling some weeds, cleaning the carpet, getting more organized. Do what you can to represent God in an excellent way.

When our children were small, we took them to Disneyland. That place was spotless. I never once saw gum stuck to the floors. Hundreds of thousands of people go through every year, and the entire park looked brand-new. I thought, *How do they do it?* One day, I saw employees going around with tools that scrape up gum. That's what they did all day long. If Disney can keep their parks that clean and that first-class, we should make God's house clean and first-class. Now apply the same standards to your own life, your house, your car, your clothes, your cubicle, and your office. I'm not talking about spending a lot of money. It's how you choose to take care of what God has given you. I'm asking you to do it with excellence.

Years ago, I was driving to the church building we occupied prior to our move into what was the Compaq Center. For some reason that day I noticed many residents in that area were not taking care of their houses. The yards weren't mowed. Weeds were everywhere. Things were stored all over the place. Not to be critical, but it just looked sloppy, one property after another. As I continued driving, I noticed in the midst of all those houses there was this one house that stood out. The lawn was mowed. The yard was immaculate. The house was painted. Everything was perfectly in place. The owners easily could have had the attitude: *Nobody else takes care of their homes, so why should we?* But they chose to have an excellent spirit. When I got to church, I commented on that house and somebody said, "Don't you know that's So-and-So's house? They're some of our most faithful members." That didn't surprise me one bit. Lakewood people are people of excellence. They stand out in the crowd. They are a cut above.

You may be in a situation today in which everybody around you is being lazy. Everybody's being sloppy. Everybody's taking the easy way out. Don't let that rub off on you. You should be the one to have an excellent spirit. You should be the one to stand out in the crowd. You may say, "Joel, you mean I bought this book so you would tell me to clean up my house?" Not just that; you should mow the lawn, too! And organize the garage while you're at it.

Seriously, what kind of example is it to your friends, your neighbors, and your coworkers if your yard is sloppy, your car is never washed, and you show up late to work? That's not a good representation, and the truth is that's not who you are. God made you as a person of excellence. Maybe all you've seen modeled is mediocrity or sloppiness, and maybe the people you work around are always late and undisciplined. But God is calling you to set a new standard. He wants to take you places higher than you've ever dreamed of, but you have to do your part and stir up the excellence inside. Don't make excuses. Don't say, "This is the way I've always been." Take this challenge and come up to a higher level of excellence.

Take Care of Yourself

Excellence applies also to your personal appearance: the way you dress and the way you present yourself. We all have different styles and different tastes. There is no right and wrong. You may not like to wear a suit, and there is nothing wrong with that. The main thing is to present yourself in a way that you're proud of. Don't go out feeling sloppy, feeling less than your best, or knowing that you didn't take the time to look like you should. You are the temple of the Most High God.

Take time to take care of yourself. Some women, in particular, take care of everyone else, putting their children first, being good wives, running the home, doing their jobs. That's good, but they need to take care of themselves, too. Get your nails done. Get your hair done. Get a massage. Go shopping. Go exercise. Go have some fun with your friends. Take care of your temple in an excellent way.

Some men haven't bought new clothes in twenty-seven years. The shirts they are wearing have been in and out of style three times already. They are taking care of their families. They are hard workers. Now they need to take care of themselves, too. When you look good, you feel better.

One time Victoria asked me to run to the grocery store and pick up something so she could finish making dinner. I had just worked out. I was hot and sweaty and wearing an old, torn-up T-shirt and run-down gym shorts. My hair wasn't combed. I looked really bad, but I didn't feel like getting cleaned up. I just jumped in the car and headed for the store, hoping I wouldn't see anyone. As I pulled into the parking lot, I heard God speak to me—not out loud, just an impression down inside—"Joel, don't you dare go in there like that. Don't you realize you are representing Me? I am the King of kings. I deserve respect and honor." I turned around and drove all the way back home, took a shower, combed my hair, put on some clean clothes, went back, and picked up those *TV dinners*. Just kidding!

Make a Habit of Excellence

When you go to a store and you accidentally knock some clothes off the rack, don't leave them on the floor and act as though you don't see them. A person of excellence picks them up and puts them back. When you're shopping for groceries and decide you don't want the box of cereal any more, don't just stick it back over by the potato chips. A person of excellence takes the cereal box back where it was found.

Well, you say, "That's what the employees are paid to do." You should do it unto God. You should do it because you have an excellent spirit. A person of excellence doesn't park in the handicap spot because it's closer to the mall entrance. A person of excellence turns off the lights in the hotel room when leaving to save energy and costs for the hotel. They don't say, "Well, I'm paying good money for that room. I don't have to do that." People of excellence go the extra mile to do what's right. They do that not because somebody is watching and not because somebody is making them. They do it to honor God.

At our house we used to have large five-gallon glass bottles of water. Each bottle had a neck, and you had to upend them and put them on this special dispenser in order to get the water out. They were not only heavy but very awkward. Victoria likes everything super clean. Because the receptor where the water goes in was completely sealed inside the bottle's neck, there's no way you can even get to it. You'd have to break the seal. But Victoria insisted that the whole bottle get wiped down with soap. When that glass had soap on it, it got very slippery, even after we dried it. I debated with her several times, saying that it wasn't necessary to wipe down the whole bottle. I was very passionate, but I couldn't convince her. So I gave Victoria my word that I would do it. But there were many times when I was in the pantry all by myself, where nobody could see me, and I would start to put that bottle up without cleaning it. Then I would hear that still small voice saying, "Joel, do the right thing. Be a person of excellence. Keep your word." More than once, I had it on the stand and had to take it down and go get the soap.

Excellence is doing the right thing even when nobody can see you. Even when you don't think it's necessary. Even when you don't agree. You gave your word, so you live up to it. Sometimes you have to say, "God, I don't feel like doing this, but I will do it unto You." Or, "I think my boss is unfair in telling me to do this, but I will do it unto You." Or, "Somebody else made the mess and I shouldn't have to clean it up, but I will do it unto You."

Pass the Small Test

Many people do not enjoy God's favor as they should because they don't pass the small tests. Being excellent may not be some huge adjustment you need to make. It may mean just leaving ten minutes earlier so you can get to work on time. It may mean not complaining when you have to clean up. It may mean not making personal phone calls on work time—just a small thing. Nobody would know it. But the Scripture says, "It's the little foxes that spoil the vines." If I had put up that water bottle week after week without cleaning it, nobody would have known except God and me. I could have gotten away with it, but here's the key: I don't want something small to keep God from releasing something big into my life.

A while back, I was in a store's parking lot, and it was very windy outside. When I opened my car door, several pieces of trash blew out on the ground. As I went to pick them up, the wind caught them and they flew about fifteen or twenty feet in different directions. I was in a hurry and didn't feel like going over to pick up those scraps. I looked around and there were already all kinds of other trash in the parking lot. I came up with several good excuses to not pick them up. I almost convinced myself to let them go, but at the last moment I decided I was going to be a person of excellence and pick up my trash. The scraps had blown here and there. As I ended up running all over that parking lot, my mind was saying, *What in the world am I doing out here? It doesn't matter. Let the stuff go.*

When I finally picked up all the scattered trash, I came back to my car. I had not realized it, but a couple was sitting in the car next to mine, watching the whole thing. They rolled the window down and said, "Hey, Joel. We watch you on television each week." Then the lady said something very interesting. "We were watching to see what you were going to do." I thought, *Oh, thank You, Jesus.*

Whether you realize it or not, people are watching you. Make sure you're representing God the right way.

Distinguish Yourself

In the Scripture, Daniel was taken away from his home in Judah and into captivity in Babylon. Even as a teenager, it says he had "an excellent spirit." He was among a group of young men in training to serve the king, and the best of them— the smartest, strongest, and most talented— would be chosen as the next leaders. They had a certain diet for them to eat and certain programs for them to follow. But Daniel had made a vow to God to always honor Him. The Babylonians worshiped idols. Daniel was respectful, but he wouldn't eat the king's fancy foods. He didn't just go along with what everyone else was doing. He made the more excellent choice.

The Scripture says, "Daniel so distinguished

himself by his exceptional qualities that the king planned to put him over the whole kingdom" (Daniel 6:3). Notice it doesn't say that God distinguished him and he got promoted. It says Daniel distinguished himself. One translation says, "Daniel completely outclassed the others." That's what happens when, number one, you honor God and, number two, you have an excellent spirit. You don't compromise. You don't just go with the flow and do what everyone else is doing. Even if everyone else is late, everyone else cuts corners, and everyone else is undisciplined, you should do as Daniel did and go the extra mile. Make the choice to be excellent.

The Scripture goes on to say Daniel was ten times wiser and more understanding than all the skilled magicians and astrologers in the realm. He could interpret dreams and visions. When you have an excellent spirit, God will give you unprecedented favor, creativity, and ideas so that, like Daniel, you will stand out in the crowd. In humility, you will outclass those who don't honor God.

My question is, Are you distinguishing your-self and not waiting for God to do it? Are you going the extra mile? Are you doing more than you have to? Are you improving your skills? Examine your life. We all have areas in which we can strive for excellence, whether it's how we treat people, how we present ourselves, or how we develop our skills. Don't let something small keep you from the big things God wants to do. You are called to be a cut above. You have excel-lence inside. It's who you are. Now do your part and be disciplined to bring out your excellence.

If you have this spirit of excellence, God will breathe in your direction and cause you to stand out. You'll be more creative, more skilled, more talented, and wiser. I believe and declare that like Daniel, you will outperform, you will outclass, and you will outshine, and God will promote you and set you in a place of honor.

2

Don't Settle for Good Enough

In Genesis 38, there is a story about a woman who was pregnant with twins. When she gave birth, one of the baby's arms came out first. The midwife tied a small cord around it, planning to gently pull him, but before she could do that, the baby pulled his arm back and his brother broke through and was born first. One stretched and one settled.

In a similar way, there are two people inside each of us. One says, "I will become everything God has created me to be. I can do all things through Christ. I'm surrounded by God's favor."

The other says, "I'll never get out of debt. The economy is too bad. I'll never lose the weight. My metabolism is off. I'll never break that addiction. I'll just learn to live with it." One wants to stretch. The other wants to settle. You can choose which person you will be. Too many people make the choice to settle. "My marriage is not what it should be, but at least we're still together. It's good enough." Or, "I don't really like this job, but at least I'm employed. It's good enough." Or, "I would love to make A's in school but I'm not that smart. These C's are good enough."

No, don't make the mistake of settling for "good enough." Good enough is not your destiny. You are a child of the Most High God. You have seeds of greatness inside. If you are to see the fullness of what God has in store, you have to have the right attitude: *I'm not letting good enough be good enough. I know I was created for greatness. I was created to excel, to live a healthy life, to overcome obstacles, to fulfill my destiny. I am not settling. I'm stretching. I'm letting go of the things that didn't work out and reaching forward to the new things God has in store.*

Maybe you have lost your fire. At one time you may have known you would break an addiction, beat a sickness, or find someone to marry, but you've gone through disappointments. Your life has not worked out the way you thought it would. Now you've accepted the fact that your vision for your life will probably not happen. You've become comfortable with good enough. But God is saying to you what He said to the people of Israel in the wilderness after the exodus from Egypt: "You have dwelt long enough on this mountain." It's time to move forward. God has new levels in front of you, new opportunities, new relationships, promotions, and breakthroughs. But you need to stir up what God put inside you, stir up the dreams and the promises you've pushed down.

You may be saying, "It's not going to happen, Joel. I'm too old. I don't have the connections. I don't know the right people." No, God has it all figured out. If you start believing again, start dreaming again, start pursuing what God put in your heart, God will make a way where you can't see a way. He will connect you to the right people. He will open doors no man can shut. What God spoke over your life, what He promised you in the night, what He whispered in your spirit, those hidden dreams, He will bring to pass.

The good news is, just because you gave up a dream doesn't mean God gave up. You may have changed your mind, but God didn't change His mind. He still has a victorious plan in front of you. Why don't you get in agreement with Him?

Don't Settle for Second Best

I read a story about a young man who dreamed of playing professional football. In high school he was a star player and won all kinds of awards. He came from a very small town where everybody knew him. All the children looked up to him as a hero and wanted to be like him. But most of the coaches thought he was too small to play in college. All the major universities turned him down. He ended up at a junior college, took a job at a pizza restaurant, and quit playing football. One night he was delivering a pizza and a ten-year-old boy answered the door. When this boy saw the young man, his eyes grew so big. The boy was starstruck. He couldn't believe this was the same person he'd watched play at the local high school, the same athlete who had thrilled the crowd so many times. After a second or two, the boy's father came to the door and the young man gave him the pizza. The little boy was very confused. He looked up at his father, then he looked at the young man and said innocently, "What are you doing delivering pizzas?"

Those words from a ten-year-old boy lit a new fire inside the young man. After work that night, he went to the gym and started training. That summer he trained harder than he had ever trained and gained seventy pounds, getting bigger, stronger, quicker, and faster. In the fall, he tried out at a major university that had accepted him as a student. He'd always wanted to play there. He made the team and kept working until he also became their star player. After college, he was drafted in the first round to play professional football and became a star in the NFL, living out his dream. But he said, "It would have never happened if that boy hadn't asked me, 'What are you doing delivering pizzas?'"

My question is, Have you settled somewhere way beneath what you know God has put in you? Have you given up on a dream or let go of a promise because it didn't happen the first time? Maybe you had a setback. Maybe somebody told you, "You're not talented enough. You're not big enough." But I ask you respectfully, "What are you doing there? You have so much in you. You are full of talent, ideas, creativity, and potential." When God breathed His life into you, He put a part of Himself in you. You have the spiritual

DNA of Almighty God. You were never created to be average, to barely get by, to always struggle, or to just have to take the leftovers. You were created as the head and not the tail.

You are equipped. Empowered. Fully loaded. Lacking nothing. Don't you dare settle for second best. Don't get stuck in a rut thinking that you've reached your limits. Draw the line in the sand and say, "That's it. I've let good enough be good enough long enough. Today is a new day. My dream may not have happened the first time I tried for it, or even the fifth time or the thirtieth time, but I'm not settling. I'm stretching my faith, looking for opportunities, taking steps to improve. I'm going to become everything God has created me to be."

When you do the natural, God will do the supernatural. When you do what you can, God will come and do what you cannot. Don't take the easy way out. Stand strong and fight the good fight of faith.

Make It All the Way

In the Scripture, Abraham is listed as one of the heroes of faith. God made one of the first covenants with him. In Genesis 12, God told Abraham to leave his country, his people, and his father's household, and He would make Abraham into a great nation. Abraham traveled to the land of Canaan, and God promised to give this land to his offspring—the Promised Land.

What's interesting is that many years before this, Abraham's father, Terah, had taken Abraham and Sarah and his grandson Lot and left their hometown of Ur, with the goal of settling in Canaan. Genesis 11 says that Abraham's father was going to the Promised Land just like God told Abraham later. But it says, "He stopped along the way and settled in Harran." Why did he stop? Were there too many difficulties? It was hard traveling with all of his flocks and herds. He had his family and their possessions. It wasn't comfortable. He finally decided, "I can't go any farther. I know this isn't the Promised Land, but it's good enough. At least we can survive out here. At least we can make it."

How many times do we do the same thing? We start off right. We have a big dream. We're fulfilling our destinies. But along the way we face opposition. Adversity arises. Too many times we say, "What's the use? I can never break this addiction. My marriage is never getting better. I'll never accomplish my dreams. I'm just settling here. It's good enough."

But I want to light a new fire in you today. You are not weak, defeated, or lacking. You have been armed with strength for every battle. That obstacle is no match for you. You have the most powerful force in the universe breathing in your direction. Don't be a weakling. Be a warrior. Your marriage is worth fighting for. Your health is worth fighting for. Your dreams and your children are worth fighting for. Dig in and say, "I am in it to win it. I know God didn't bring me this far to leave me here. I'm not settling halfway, three-fourths of the way, or nine-tenths of the way. I will make it all the way into my promised land."

If you're to be victorious, you must have a made-up mind. Be determined. You can't give up when life becomes difficult. You can't complain because it's taking a long time. You can't be discouraged because you went through a setback. Everything God promised you is worth fighting for, so you need to be in it for the long haul. You may need to pull up your stakes. You camped and settled halfway like Abraham's father. You have become comfortable and decided that your dreams will never come to pass, your health will never improve, or you'll never get out of debt. I'm asking you to pack up your tent, gather up your belongings, and start moving forward. You may have hit a temporary delay, but that's okay. That won't stop you from fulfilling your destiny. Today can be your new beginning. God is breathing new life into your spirit. He has greater victories in front of you. Get a vision for it.

"This sounds good, Joel, but I'll never meet the right person. I'll never earn the promotion at work. I'll never break this addiction." Every time you dwell on those negative, discouraging thoughts, you are stopping short of your promised land. The first place we lose the battle is in our thinking. If you don't think you can be successful, you never will be. If you don't think you can overcome the past, or meet the right person, or accomplish your dreams, you'll be stuck right where you are. You have to change your thinking. The Creator of the universe is arranging things in your favor. He said no good thing would He withhold because you walk uprightly. He will not withhold the right person, the wisdom, the breaks, or the turnaround.

An A Is Worth Fighting For

I read about a university professor who was giving his students their most important test of the year.

Before he gave them the test, he told his students he was proud of them because they had worked so hard. Then he made them a special offer. He said, "Anyone who would like an automatic C on this test, just raise your hand and I'll give you a C. You won't even have to take the test." One hand slowly went up, then another and another, until about half the students opted out of taking the test. They walked out of the room so relieved and happy.

The professor next passed out the test forms to the rest of the students. He placed a form face down on each desk, then he asked the students not to turn their forms over until he told them to begin. For the next few minutes he gave them encouragement, saying they would do great things in life and how they should always strive to do their best. Then he told them to turn over the test forms and begin. But when they looked at the test, there were only two sentences: "Congratulations. You just made an A."

Too many times, like the first group of

students, we settle for a C when God has an A for us. If you say you will never recover from an illness, that's taking a C. You need to change your thinking and say, "God is restoring health to me. I will live and not die. I'm getting stronger, healthier, better." That's going for the A. Or, "I know this guy I'm dating is not good for me. He doesn't treat me right, but I may never meet anybody else." That's not a C. That's a D!

God has an A, but you'll never see it if you keep taking the C's. Yes, the C's are easier. You don't have to stretch. You don't have to leave your comfort zone. But you'll never be truly fulfilled if you keep settling for C's. The good news is God already has A's in your future. He has the right person, a happy marriage, a successful career, health, wholeness, freedom, and victory.

Don't take the easy way out. The A's are worth fighting for. I can't think of much that would be sadder than to come to the end of life and have to wonder, *What could I have become if I didn't settle for good enough? What could I have been if I didn't take so many C's but instead I pressed forward, striving to be my very best?*

You may have taken some C's in the past. We all have. But make a decision with me that from now on you're only going for the A's.

Good Can Be the Enemy of Great

Here's a key: If you're not seeing the things in your life that God promised in your spirit, keep moving forward. It's only temporary. Like the young man delivering pizzas, you may be doing something that's below your potential, working at a job in which you're not using your gifts. Don't slack off when you're there. Keep being your best, but see that as only temporary. You are just passing through. Don't put your stakes down. Don't settle there. If the medical report doesn't agree with what God says about you, don't accept it as the way it will always be. Your attitude should be:

This is just a season I'm passing through. I'm coming into health, wholeness, and victory.

Maybe God has blessed you with good things, such as a great family, a wonderful job, and good health. You've seen His favor. But you know there are greater levels in front of you. It's easy to think, *I'm happy. I have no complaints. God has been good to me.* But I've learned that good can be the enemy of great. Don't let that be an excuse to keep you from God's best. Stir up your greatness. Stretch into a new level.

This is where the people of Israel missed it. God brought them out of slavery in Egypt. They were headed toward the Promised Land, a land flowing with milk and honey. The spies sent into the land came back and said, "Moses, we have never seen such a magnificent land, so beautiful, luscious, green." The fruits and vegetables were like nothing they had experienced. It took two people to carry a single cluster of grapes on a pole. That was the vision God had in front of them. That was the A.

In the wilderness they saw God's goodness. They saw God part the Red Sea, bring water out of a rock, and rain down manna from Heaven. But do you know that was all only temporary provision? That was only the C. The mistake they made was that when they came to the Promised Land, there were enemies living on it. All the people of Israel had to do was fight for the land. God had promised them the victory, but they were not willing to fight. They thought, *It's not worth it. It's too much trouble to take the fortified cities. Besides, those people are bigger than us, and there are giants.* I believe one reason they settled for the C so easily is because they had seen God's favor in the wilderness. They thought, *It's not so bad out here. God takes care of us. He feeds us and provides water. We've been safe. It's good enough.* They were too easily satisfied. They didn't realize everything God had done up to that point was only temporary provision. It was to sustain them until they reached their land of abundance.

You can probably say, as I can, that you've

seen God be good to you. God has blessed you with health, a family, and a job. He has opened doors that should not have opened. He has shown you favor and protected you. Can I tell you that these were only temporary provisions? You have not made it into your promised land. God is taking you somewhere greater than you've ever imagined. The Scripture says, "No eye has seen, no ear has heard, no mind has imagined the amazing things God has in store for those who love the Lord."

Don't make the mistake made by the people of Israel when they built houses where they should have pitched tents. Don't let your temporary provision become permanent. Yes, God has been good to you, but you haven't seen anything yet. What God has in your future will supersede what you've seen in the past. Thank God for His goodness. Be grateful for the Red Sea's parting. Thank Him for the protection, the provision, and the favor. But if it's not what God put in your spirit, be bold enough to pick up your stakes and say,

"God, this is all great. You've been awesome in my life, and I thank You for it. But I believe this is only temporary provision. Where You're taking me is to a land of abundance, a place like I've never experienced before." That's not being selfish. That's releasing your faith for the fullness of your destiny.

A Thousand Times More

We have to let the promises that God spoke to the Israelites sink down into our spirit. "I will give you houses that you didn't have to build. You will reap from vineyards that you did not plant." One version adds, "May the God of your fathers make you a thousand times more than you are." I don't know about you, but I can't settle where I am right now. I have to pull up my stakes. God has a thousand times more for us: more joy, more peace, more influence, more wisdom, more ideas, more creativity, and more good breaks. Take the limits off God.

When Joshua was leading the people of Israel, God said, "Joshua, you have not passed this way before." God is saying the same thing to us. Something out of the ordinary is coming your way—new levels of favor, unprecedented opportunities, divine connections. God has A's in your future. People are already lined up to be good to you. You don't have to find them. They'll come find you. When you honor God, His blessings will chase you down. You won't be able to outrun the good things of God.

My challenge to you is this: Don't settle where you are in your health, your relationships, your career, or your walk with the Lord. Keep stretching. Keep growing. Keep believing. Keep dreaming. Don't let good enough be good enough. Be determined to become everything God created you to be. You may have dwelled on that same mountain long enough. It's time to pull up your stakes. Pack up your belongings. Start moving forward. Enlarge your vision. Make room in your thinking for the new thing God wants to do. Don't let your temporary provision become permanent.

If you learn this principle of stretching and not settling, you will see the fullness of what God has in store. I believe you will overcome obstacles and accomplish dreams. Not like Abraham's father but like Joshua, you're going to make it all the way to your promised land.

3

Keep Growing

Too many people suffer from destination disease. They reach a certain level, earn their degrees, buy their dream homes, and then just coast. Studies show that 50 percent of high school graduates never read another entire book. One reason may be that they see learning as something you do in school, just something you do for a period of life instead of as a way of life.

We all learned when we were in school. Our teachers, coaches, and parents taught us. We were expected to learn when we were school age. But some tend to think that once they finish a certain level of education: "I'm done with school. I've finished my training. I have a good job." But winners never stop learning. This is an undeniable quality of people of excellence. God did not create us to reach one level and then stop. Whether you're nine or ninety years old, you should constantly be learning, improving your skills, and getting better at what you do.

You have to take responsibility for your own growth. Growth is not automatic. What steps are you taking to improve? Are you reading books or listening to educational videos or audios? Are you taking any courses on the Internet or at your local college? Are you going to seminars? Do you have mentors? Are you gleaning information from people who know more than you?

People of excellence don't coast through life relying on what they have already learned. You have treasure inside—gifts, talents, and potential put in you by the Creator of the universe. But those gifts will not automatically come out. They must be developed.

Grow Your Gifts

I read that the wealthiest places on Earth are not the oil fields of the Middle East or the diamond mines of South Africa. The wealthiest places are the cemeteries. Buried in the ground are businesses that were never formed, books that were never written, songs that were never sung, dreams that never came to life, potential that was never released. Don't go to your grave with that buried treasure. Keep growing. Keep learning. Every day we should have a goal to grow in some way, to learn something new.

Pablo Casals was one of the greatest cellists of all time. He started playing at the age of twelve and accomplished feats that no other cellist did. He was known around the world as the greatest in his field. Yet, at the age of eighty-five, Casals still practiced five hours a day. A reporter asked him why he still put so much effort into it. He smiled and said, "I think I'm getting better."

Casals understood this principle: When you stop learning, you stop growing. Whatever you do, get better at it. Sharpen your skills. Don't be at the same level next year as you are right now. Like the great cellist, get better. Get excellent.

There are all kinds of opportunities to increase. There is more knowledge available today than at any other time in history. You have no excuse for not improving. You don't have to go to the library or even travel to a university. With the Internet, information flows right into your home. The Internet wasn't created just to share pictures, play games, or chat with friends. That's all fine, but the Internet is a tool that can help you increase your gifts.

You have a responsibility not only to God, not only to your family, but also to yourself to develop what He's put in you. If you're in sales, human resources, auto mechanics, or health care, you can always expand your knowledge and improve your skills. No matter what you do, there are experts who have gone where you're

trying to go. Listen to what they have to say.
Read books to learn how to communicate, work
as a team member, or lead more effectively. Take
twenty minutes a day, turn off the TV, and invest
in yourself.

You should be doing something intentional
and strategic every day to improve your skills.
Don't be vague in your approach. Do not say, "If
I have time, I'll do it." You are better than that.
You have too much in you to stay where you
are. Your destiny is too great to get stuck. A lot
of times we sit back and think, *God, I'm waiting on You. I'm waiting for that big break.* Let me
tell you who gets the big breaks—people who are
prepared, those who develop their skills continu-
ously. You have to be proactive to take steps to
grow. When God sees you doing your part and
developing what He's given you, He'll do His
part and open up doors that no man can shut.

You may be tempted to say, "Well, Joel, I'm
so busy. I don't have time to take any training
courses. I don't have time to read books, to learn

new things. I'll get behind." That's the wrong attitude. It's like two lumberjacks who were out chopping down trees. One said, "I'm going to take a break and go sharpen my axe." The other said, "I don't have time to stop. I have too much work to do. Sharpening my axe will put me behind." He kept chopping and chopping. The other man came back three hours later with a sharpened axe and chopped down twice as many trees as his friend with the dull axe. Sometimes you need to take a break and sharpen your axe. If you sharpen your skills, you won't need to work as hard. If you sharpen your skills, you'll get more done in less time. You will be more productive.

Don't Settle

Whether you are a teacher, a carpenter, a banker, or a doctor, don't settle where you are. Don't coast or rest on your laurels. Stir up what God has put in you and get better at it. Sharpen your axe. This is a call to action. There are new levels in your future. Things have shifted in your favor. God is looking for people who are prepared and taking steps to improve. He is looking for those who are serious about fulfilling their destinies.

Think about David in the Scripture. He was out in the shepherds' fields taking care of his father's sheep. In today's terms, he had a boring minimum wage job and no friends, and it didn't look as though there was any opportunity for growth. Meanwhile, David's brothers got the good jobs. Three of them were in the army. That was prestigious. They were admired and respected. David could have slacked off, been sloppy, unmotivated, and thought, *There's no reason to develop my skills. I have no opportunity. I'm stuck out here with these sheep.* Instead, while he was alone, he did not sit around bored and waste time. He practiced using his sling day after day and month after month. I can envision him setting up a target, slinging rocks again and again, learning, getting better, making adjustments, and sharpening his skills. When a coyote or another predator came after his sheep, no problem for David. He would get that sling out and nail it. He was like a sharpshooter, a marksman, so precise, so skillful; he could hit a bull's-eye from a hundred meters away.

When God sought somebody to defeat a giant, somebody to lead His chosen people, He looked to see who was prepared. He wanted someone who had developed his skills, who had taken the time to cultivate the gifts He had put in him. He didn't choose just anybody. He selected a skilled marksman who could hit a target with precision. He selected a shepherd who would care for His people.

In the same way, when God seeks somebody to promote, He doesn't just randomly close His eyes and say, "I'll pick this one. You won the lottery. It's your lucky day." No, God looks for people who have developed their skills. When we read about David running toward Goliath and slinging that rock, sometimes we think it was all God's hand at work. In a sense it was God, but the truth is, God didn't sling the rock. God didn't cause the rock to hit Goliath in just the right place. It was David who developed and used the skills God gave him.

Like David, God has put in you a set of special skills that will slay giant challenges, open new doors, and thrust you to new levels. But here's the key: Your skills have to be developed. Every day you spend learning, growing, and improving will prepare you for that new level.

Prepare Yourself to Be a Winner

You may be in a lower-position job, doing something that seems insignificant. But you know you have so much more in you. It would be easy to slack off and think, *There's no future here. I'll prepare as soon as I get out of this place, when good breaks come my way, or when the boss promotes me. Maybe then I'll take some courses, lose a few pounds, have a better attitude, and buy some nicer clothes.*

That's backward. You have to start improving right where you are. Start sharpening your skills while you're waiting. Study your manager's work habits. Study your best supervisor. Learn how to do their jobs. Be ready to step into those shoes. When God sees you prepare yourself, He opens new doors. The Scripture says, "A man's gift makes room for him." If no new doors are opening, don't be discouraged. Just develop your gifts in a new way. Improve your skills. You might feel that your supervisors aren't going anywhere right now, but if you outgrow them, outperform them, outproduce them, and know more than them, your gifts will make room for you. Somewhere, somehow, and some way God will open a door and get you where He wants you to be. Don't worry about who is ahead of you or when your time will come. Just keep growing, learning, and preparing. When you are ready, the right doors will open.

The fact is, God may not want you to have

your supervisor's position. That may be too low for you. He may want to thrust you right past your boss and put you at a whole new level. I know former receptionists who went from answering the phones to running multimillion-dollar companies. Develop what's in you, and you'll go further than you can imagine.

You Were Created to Increase

Have you come down with destination disease? You're comfortable, not learning anything new. But you have so much more in you. Studies tell us that the average person only uses 11 percent of his or her brain. Think of all that potential you could be tapping into. Maybe you're an accountant. That's good, but don't settle there. Why not get your CPA certification? That is a new skill you can develop. That gift will make more room for you.

Maybe you're an electrician, a plumber, or a

mechanic. That's great, but what steps are you taking to improve your skills and your position in life? If you spend two hours a day improving on the same skills, in three years you will be an expert in that area. Find what you're good at and keep improving on it. In today's competitive marketplace, with the economy so tight and businesses so bottom-line oriented, if you're not improving, you're falling behind. If your skill levels are at the same place today they were five years ago, you're at a disadvantage.

I want to light a new fire under you. Shake off that destination disease. Sharpen your skills. I read an article about reducing the risk of being laid off. It said there are three main things that employers look for in determining who stays. They look for people with positive attitudes, flexibility, and the desire to keep learning and improving.

To be a winner, you need to develop your gifts to the point where your company can't make it without you. Or at least you want your boss to know things don't run nearly as smoothly when you're gone. If you're out for a week and nobody misses you—sales are just as good, all the work gets done—that's okay as long as you own the company. But if you're an employee, that's alarming. If you're not being missed, maybe you're not needed. You need to kick it into a new gear. Produce more than you've been producing. Take some classes to increase your skills. Step it up a notch. Don't settle for a low position where no one will miss you. You have treasure in you. There is talent and skill that will cause you to be noticed. The writer of Proverbs says, "Do you see a person skilled in their work? They will stand before kings and great men." Keep sharpening your skills. Cream always rises to the top.

This is what Joseph did in the Bible. When he was sold into slavery by his brothers and taken to Egypt, he started off at the very bottom. But Joseph didn't wait for vindication. Even as a slave, he decided to be his best and develop his gifts. Joseph made himself so valuable that he was put in charge of his master's household. When he was falsely accused and put in prison, he was so organized, so wise, and so skillful that they put him in charge of the whole prison.

Joseph was cream rising to the top. His use of his gift of interpreting dreams brought him before Pharaoh and made a big impression. When Pharaoh needed someone to run the country and administer the nationwide food program, Pharaoh didn't choose one of his department heads or a cabinet member. He chose Joseph— a prisoner and a foreigner. Why? Joseph developed his skills right where he was, and his gifts made room for him. Don't use where you are as an excuse to not grow. Don't say, "I'm not in a good job. I don't like my position. I've had unfair things happen. That's why I've lost my passion."

Remember, the treasure is still in you. God is saying it's time to use your gifts. Stretch yourself. Take some courses. Sharpen your skills. You should be so productive, so filled with wisdom that no matter where you are, like Joseph, you will rise to the top.

Be the Solution, Not the Problem

One way you'll be invaluable is by learning to be a problem solver. That's what Joseph was. He was solution-oriented. Don't go to your boss and say, "Our department is falling apart. This manager is about to quit. Bob cursed out Jim, and Bill keeps leaving early. Nobody paid our taxes last month. What are you going to do?" That's not the way to get promoted. If you present a problem, always present a solution as well. If you can't present a solution, hold it until you can figure out something.

A child can tell me the building is on fire. That's easy. That doesn't take any skill. But I want somebody to tell me that not only is the building on fire, but the fire department is on the way, all the people are safe, the insurance company has been notified, and temporary quarters have been arranged. If you want to be invaluable to your organization, present your bosses with solutions, not problems.

What steps are you taking to better yourself so you can go to the next level? Are you reading books and trade magazines to stay up to date? Can you take a course to gain an advantage? You have to be on the offensive, even if you have your degree. Do you know many degrees are outdated in as little as five years? I was talking to an airline pilot who told me that pilots must go every year to update their training so they can continue flying. Why? The technology changes so fast. The world is changing so fast. If you don't continue learning and keep growing, you will fall behind.

Don't come down with destination disease. Break out of that box and learn something new. Will Rogers said, "Even if you're on the right track, you'll get run over if you just sit there." If you don't take steps to keep growing, don't be surprised if someone comes along and takes the promotion that belongs to you. God has new levels in your future, but if you're not prepared for them—if you haven't developed the treasure He's put in you—you can miss out on the fullness of what He has in store.

Every one of us should have a personal growth plan. Not something vague: "I'll read a book every once in a while. I'll take the company training when I have time." No, you need a specific plan that lays out how you're going to grow. It should include the steps you will take to get better. Let me give you some ideas. The average American spends three hundred hours a year in a car. That's valuable time. Imagine what you can learn in three hundred hours. Take advantage of it. Instead of listening to the radio driving to and from work, turn your car into a university. Listen to teaching audiobooks and CDs. Listen to training materials and to other helpful material that will help you grow and improve in your field. You can also listen to inspiring and informative audios while working out. I have people tell me all the time, "Joel, I listen to you while I run. I listen to you at the gym." One lady said, "I listen to you every night before I go to bed. You always put me right to sleep." I thought, *Thanks a lot!*

People of Excellence Do the Little Things That Count

There are all kinds of simple things people do to keep growing and bettering themselves. You don't have to spend three hours a day studying. Just take advantage of the time you're not using right now. Podcasts are a great tool. You can download messages and listen to them whenever you want. We have given away millions of copies of my messages at no charge. That's a growth plan.

If you want to keep growing, you need to have good mentors, people who have been where you want to go, people who know more than you. Let them speak into your life. Listen to their ideas. Learn from their mistakes. Study how they think and how they got to where they are.

I heard about a company that held a sales class for several hundred employees. The speaker asked if anyone knew the names of their top three salespeople. Every person raised a hand. He then asked: How many of them had gone to lunch with these top salespeople and taken time to find out how they do what they do? Not one hand went up. There are people all around us whom God put in our paths on purpose so we can gain wisdom, insight, and experience, but we have to be open to learning from them. Look around and find the winners you could learn from.

I say this respectfully: Don't waste your valuable time with people who aren't contributing to your growth. Life is too short for you to hang around people who are not going anywhere. Destination disease is contagious. If you're with them long enough, their lack of ambition and energy will rub off on you. People of excellence need to associate with inspiring people who build you up, people who challenge you to go higher, not anyone who pulls you down and convinces you to settle where you are. Your destiny is too important for that.

Build a Foundation for Continuous Growth

Young people often get caught up in trying to be popular instead of trying to be their best. I've found that in twenty years nobody will care whether you were popular in high school. Those who need attention and act up and don't study because it isn't cool will find things change after high school. What matters is having a good education, good work habits, and a good attitude that gives you a foundation to build on. Popularity is about wanting people to like you, but happiness is about liking yourself. In most schools, the science and engineering fairs are not the most popular events. Being in the math club isn't nearly as cool as being on the football team. Some of my friends made fun of people on the debate team, but now they work for people who were on the debate team.

Junior high and high school are critical times in our lives and our formative years. There's so much emphasis on studies. I loved and played sports when I was growing up, and I still do. They teach discipline and teamwork and perseverance, and that's all great. But we need to keep sports in perspective. Most of us are not going to play sports for a living. One in one million kids will play professional basketball. The average professional football career is three and a half years. Even if you do make it, you still need a good foundation for life after football. When you study and learn and take school seriously, you may be called a bookworm, a geek, or a nerd, but don't worry about those names. In a few years, you'll be called the boss. You'll be called CEO, president, senator, pastor, or doctor.

Three of the most influential businessmen and inventors of the early 1900s, Thomas Edison, Henry Ford, and Harvey Firestone, had winter homes next to each other in Florida. They were close friends and spent much of their winters together. Who you associate with makes a difference in how far you go in life. If your friends are Larry, Curly, and Moe, you may have fun, but you may not be going anywhere. The Scripture says, "We should redeem the time." You need to see time as a gift. God has given us 86,400 seconds each day. You're not being responsible with what God gave you if you're hanging out with time wasters who have no goals and no dreams. You have a destiny to fulfill. God has amazing things in your future. It's critical that you surround yourself with the right people. If you're the smartest one in your group, your group is too small. You need to be around people who know more than you and have more talent than you. Don't be intimidated by them; be inspired.

If you take an oak tree seed and plant it in a

five-gallon pot, the tree will never grow to the size it was created to be. Why? It's restricted by the size of the pot. In the same way, God has created you to do great things. He's put talent, ability, and skills inside. You don't want to be restricted by your environment. It may be too small. The people you hang around with may think small or be negative and drag you down. You need to get out of that little pot because God created you to soar. It's fine to help people in need, but don't spend all your time with them. You need talented and smart people in your life; winners who are further along than you and can inspire you and challenge you to rise higher.

My question is, Are you doing anything strategic and intentional to keep growing? If not, you can start right now. Come up with a personal growth plan. It can be something like, "I will get up every morning and spend the first twenty minutes meditating on the Scripture. I will listen to a teaching CD driving to work. I will read a book for fifteen minutes every night before I go to bed. I will meet with my mentor twice a month. I will be in church every weekend."

That's a definite plan. When you take responsibility for your growth, God will honor your efforts. Promotion, good breaks, businesses, books, and divine connections are in your future. But now is the time to prepare. Don't get caught with destination disease.

There is treasure in you, waiting to be developed. Redeem the time. Make a decision to grow in some way every day. If you keep sharpening your skills and getting better, God promises your gifts will make room for you. Like David, because you are prepared, I believe and declare God is about to thrust you into the fullness of your destiny. He will open doors that no man can shut. You will go further than you could imagine and become the person of excellence He's created you to be.

4

Stay Focused

Time is one of the most valuable commodities we have. It's more valuable than money. You can make more money, but you can't make more time. As I noted in the previous chapter, the Scripture tells us to redeem the time. That means don't waste it. Don't live this day unfocused, undisciplined, and unmotivated. We have a responsibility to use our time wisely. We're not always going to be here. This day is a gift. Are you living it to the full? With purpose and passion? Pursuing your dreams? Or are you distracted? Indifferent? Just doing whatever comes along? Are you in a job you don't like? Hanging out with people who are pulling you down? That's not redeeming the time; that's wasting the time. Just like you spend money, you are spending your life. You're either investing it or you're wasting it.

The first step is to set short-term and long-term goals. What do you want to accomplish this week? What do you want to be five years from now? Do you have a plan? Are you taking steps to get there? Don't go another three years on a job you don't like, doing something that you're not passionate about. Life is flying by. This is your one shot. You don't get a do-over. We can't relive our twenties or thirties. Once this day is over, we can never get it back.

The apostle Paul says in Ephesians, "Make the most of every opportunity. Don't be vague and thoughtless, but live purposefully and accurately." If you're going to reach your highest potential, you have to be an "on purpose" person. You know where you're going. You're not vague, distracted, waiting to see what happens. You're focused. You're making the most of each opportunity. Let me put it in more practical terms: Staying on social media for hours a day and catching up on the latest gossip is not redeeming the time. Playing video games for hours a day when you could be studying is not redeeming the time. Talking on the phone for hours to a friend who's not going anywhere and has no dreams is not redeeming the time.

God has given you a present. It's called "today." What are you going to do with it? This is a call to action. Get focused. Get organized. Set your goals. Make your plans. God could have chosen anyone to be here, but He chose you.

Live a Well-Spent Life

The Scripture talks about living well-spent lives, excellent lives. When we go to bed at night, we should ask ourselves, "Did I live a well-spent day? Did I take steps toward my goals? Was I a blessing to someone else? Did I invest my time or waste my time?" I read that the average person spends over eighty hours a year looking for things they misplaced—car keys, cell phones, glasses, receipts, and children! Somebody said that the reason God gives babies to young people is because older people would forget where they left them. Do yourself a favor—save yourself eighty hours a year and get organized. Redeem that time.

I know too many people who are incredibly talented and have great potential, but they're not disciplined when it comes to how they spend their time. They have good intentions, but they're easily distracted and end up off course. There are a thousand good things you can give your time to each day. You have to be disciplined to stay focused on what's best for you. If not, you'll end up chasing the latest trend, trying to keep up with your friends, distracted, entangled in things that are not a part of your destiny.

I heard about a man who was walking

through the airport on the way to his departure
gate. He saw a sign on the terminal wall that said,
"Know your future, 25 cents." He was intrigued
by it, so he walked over and put a quarter in the
slot. The computer readout said, "Your name is
John Smith. You're on the 2:20 flight to Boston."
He couldn't believe it. He thought, *How does this
thing know my name? How does it know my flight?*
A friend was walking by, so he called him over
and said, "Look at this." He put in another quarter. It did it again. "Your name is John Smith.
You're on the 2:20 flight to Boston." His friend
looked puzzled, shrugged his shoulders, and
went on. The man reached in his pocket to get
another quarter out and try it again, but he didn't
have any more coins. He had to walk way back
to the newsstand to get change. There was a long
line, and he waited and waited. He finally got a
quarter, came back, and put it in the slot. It said,
"Your name is John Smith. You just *missed* the
2:20 flight to Boston."

Stay focused. It's easy to get sidetracked by

things that pull you off course, and when you finally look up, the day is gone, or the year is gone, or twenty years are gone. Nothing will be sadder than to come to the end of life and think, *Why did I waste so many days? Why didn't I live focused?* Make this decision with me that you're going to redeem the time. We have a responsibility. God has entrusted you with His life. He breathed His breath into you. He's put gifts and talents inside. You have seeds of greatness. You're not just on Planet Earth taking up space. You're a person of destiny. With that gift of life comes a responsibility to develop your talents, to pursue your dreams, and to become who God created you to be.

Make Sure You Are Running with Purpose

On a regular basis, you need to reevaluate what you're doing. Refocus your life. Get rid of any distractions. Paul said in another place, "I run

with purpose in every step." When we understand the value of time and see each day as the
gift that it is, it helps us to keep the right perspective. You realize every battle is not worth fighting.
You don't have time to get engaged in conflicts
that are not between you and your God-given
destiny. If somebody has a problem with you, as
long as you're being your best, doing what God's
put in your heart, with all due respect, that's their
problem and not yours. You don't have to resolve
conflicts with every person. Some people don't
want to be at peace with you. That's a distraction.
Don't waste your valuable time fighting battles
that don't matter.

When you realize your days are numbered,
you don't respond to every critic. You don't try to
convince people to like you who are never going
to like you. You accept the fact that some people
are never going to give you their approval. But
that's okay. You know you have Almighty God's
approval. When you're redeeming the time,
you're not trying to keep someone happy who's

never going to be happy. With some people, no matter what you do for them, it's not going to be enough. But their happiness is not your responsibility. Always be kind and respectful, but your attitude should be: *If you don't want to be happy, that's fine, but you're not going to keep me from being happy. I know this day is a gift, and I'm not going to live it trying to change things that I cannot change or trying to fix people who don't want to be fixed.* That's redeeming the time.

When you realize your time is limited, you don't get offended. You don't get upset because somebody's playing politics in the office. You don't get stressed out because somebody's trying to make you look bad. You let it go and trust God to make your wrongs right.

A lady told me about a family member who had done her wrong. She was very negative and starting to get bitter. I told her what I'm telling you. Life is too short for you to live that way. Let it go, and God will be your vindicator. She didn't want to hear it. She said, "No, I'm not going to be happy until he apologizes." What she doesn't realize is that she is wasting valuable days. He may never apologize. I wonder how many days that we've wasted doing similar things. We can't say that we redeemed the time; we didn't appreciate the day. We just dragged through it being upset, offended, and discouraged.

The Scripture says, "Don't let the sun go down on your anger." The reason many people have no joy or enthusiasm is because they go to bed each night with unforgiveness in their heart. They're reliving their hurts, thinking about their disappointments. Here's the problem: If the sun goes down with bitterness, it will come back up with bitterness. If it goes down with resentment, it comes back up with resentment. That's blocking God's blessings. It's keeping you from seeing the bright future. If you want the sun to shine brightly in your life once again, before you go to bed each night, you need to say, "God, I'm releasing every negative thing that's happened to me today. I'm releasing every hurt, releasing every worry, releasing every disappointment. I'm forgiving the people who did me wrong. God, I'm going to bed in peace." When you do that, the sun will go down with nothing blocking it. When it comes back up the next morning, you'll have a new spring in your step because you're excited about the day and ready for your future. Don't go to bed at night with any kind of defeat still in your mind.

Invest Your Time Wisely

I talked to a young television reporter at a local station in Houston. During Hurricane Ike in 2008, she was out covering the story. Her assignment was to find people who were down-and-out and having a hard time finding food because of the hurricane. She was at one of the food drops, talking to people in line, but nobody had a sad story. They were all grateful that they were alive and talking about how they were going to make it. Victoria and I and some Lakewood volunteers happened to be there. She came over with the camera and asked me, "What's the worst thing that you've seen?" I said, "Yes, some people are struggling, but they have faith; they're overcomers. They know they're victors and not victims." She thought, *Well, I knew Joel wasn't going to tell me anything sad.* So she went and found Victoria, who was worse than me. She said, "These people are fired up. They know God's in control, and something better is coming their way."

When the reporter got back to the station, she told her supervisor, "I couldn't find any sad stories, but I got Joel and Victoria Osteen to comment on the hurricane." She thought they would be excited, but it was just the opposite. They didn't want us; they wanted sad stories. She ended up getting terminated over that incident. They let her go! She could have been discouraged, depressed, and bitter, but she understood this principle that every day is a gift from God. She started thanking God that new doors were going to open and thanking Him that favor was coming her way. Not long after that, she received a phone call from a very prestigious broadcasting company. They saw her report on the hurricane—the same one that got her fired. They said, "We'd like to offer you a full-time position to come and head up the department that does all our documentaries." That was a dream come true. She couldn't believe it. She gave me a big hug and said, "Joel, I want to thank you and Victoria for getting me fired."

I've heard it said, "Disappointments are inevitable, but misery is optional." No matter what kind of setbacks you face, no matter who does you wrong, you don't have to drag through life defeated, depressed, and bitter. Start redeeming the time. Do as she did. Start thanking God that He's in control. Thank Him that new doors are opening. Thank Him that favor is coming your way. The truth is that we all go through the valleys, but the valleys are what lead us to higher mountains. They're not permanent; they're only temporary. Here's a key: When you're in the valley, instead of sitting around thinking about your problems, go out and do something good for somebody else. Volunteer while you're in the valley. Usher while you're in the valley. Cheer somebody up while you're in the valley. Mow somebody's lawn while you're in the valley. When you invest your time the right way in helping others, those seeds that you sow will create the harvest you need, not to just get out of the valley, but to come to a higher mountain, to come up to a new level of your destiny.

Reevaluate Who You Spend Your Time With

It's not only important how we spend our time, but with whom we spend it. To redeem the time may mean you have to prune some relationships that are not adding value to your life. Don't hang around people who are not going anywhere, who have no goals or dreams. People who are not focused and not disciplined. They compromise and take the easy way out. If you tolerate mediocrity, it will rub off on you. If you hang out with jealous, critical, unhappy people, you will end up jealous, critical, and unhappy. That's what it says in Proverbs: "Walk with the wise and become wise; associate with fools and get in trouble."

Take a look at your friends. That's what you're going to be like in a few years. If your friends are winners, leaders, givers, and successful, if they have integrity and a spirit of excellence and are positive and motivated, those good qualities are going to rub off on you. When you're with them, you're investing your time. They're making you better. But if you hang out with people who are sloppy, undisciplined, not motivated, and not going anywhere, let me give you some great advice: Find some new friends. You cannot become who God created you to be hanging out with them. They may be good people, and they may have good hearts, but your destiny is too great, your assignment is too important, and your time is too valuable to let them drag you down.

The only thing that's keeping some people from a new level of their destiny is wrong friendships. You cannot hang out with chickens and expect to soar like an eagle. You don't have to make some big announcement and go tell them, "Hey, I'm cutting you off. Joel said to get rid of you." No, do me a favor and leave my name out of this. But you can just gradually spend less and less time with them. "Well, what if I hurt their feelings?" Well, what if they keep you from your destiny?

I heard about a lady who was reevaluating her friendships. Her voicemail recording said, "I'm sorry I missed your call. I'm making some changes in my life. If I don't call you back, please know you were one of those changes." I'm thinking about all the people who haven't called me back!

But here's the key: If you don't let go of the

wrong people, you'll never meet the right people. Sometimes we can outgrow a friendship. It
was good at one time. For a few years, you were
fulfilled. But now you've grown more than they
have. You're running at a different pace. Your
gifts are coming out in a greater way. That doesn't
make them a bad person. It's just a new season.
Human nature likes to hold on to the old. We
like to keep everything the same. But the truth is
that it's healthy for seasons to change. It doesn't
mean you can't still be their friend; you just know
you cannot spend as much time with them and
become all you were created to be.

There are people who come into our lives who
are like scaffolding. They're designed to be there
for a period of time. And I'm not talking about
a marriage situation; I'm talking about friendships. These people are for a period of time in our
lives. They help us grow, inspire us, and motivate
us. But like that scaffolding, at some point, it's
got to come off the building. If the scaffolding
stayed up, the building would never be what

it was meant to be. Appreciate the people who have helped you. Always honor them, but be big enough to recognize when their part in your story is over. On a regular basis, you need to reevaluate your friendships and the people with whom you choose to spend time. Are they in the right position? Has the position changed? Could it be that it's a new season?

Be Careful Who You Allow into Your Inner Circle

When Jesus was on the Earth, He was very selective with His friendships. Many people wanted to be close to Him. But He chose only twelve disciples with whom to spend most of His time. Out of those twelve, three were his close friends: Peter, James, and John. John could have been considered His best friend. He was described as the disciple whom Jesus loved. You may know a lot of people and have many acquaintances, but you have to be careful who you allow in your inner circle. You can't have twenty best friends. The higher you go and the more successful you are, the tighter your circle needs to become. You may have twenty people you call friends, and that's great. But make sure the two or three you choose to be close to you are 100 percent for you. Make sure they believe in you, stick up for you, and are with you through thick or thin. It could be that you're not seeing God's best because your team is weak. You're investing valuable time in people who were never supposed to be a part of your inner circle. If your team is weak, you're going to be weak.

In Mark 5, Jesus was traveling to another city to pray for a little girl who had died. When He arrived at the home, the Scripture states that Jesus didn't allow anyone to go in with Him except for Peter, James, and John. His inner circle. Why? Jesus knew when He got in that room where the little girl was dead, He needed people who wouldn't question who He was. He needed people who wouldn't ask, "Are You sure You're the Son of God? What if she doesn't get healed? Do You have a backup plan?"

When you're in the heat of the battle, when you need God's favor, when you need a break-through, when you need a legal situation to turn around, you cannot afford to have people in your inner circle asking, "Do you really think you're going to get well? My grandmother died of that same thing. Do you really think you're going to get out of debt? Business is so slow." You need people who are joined in spirit with you. You need people who will say, "If you're bold enough to believe it, count on me. I'm bold enough to agree with you." "If you believe you can break that addiction, I'm not going to tell you ten rea-sons why you can't. My report is, you are well able." "If you believe you can get your degree, or you can start that business, or you can see your marriage restored, count on me. I'm on board. I'm all for you."

You need people who will join faith with you

and not try to talk you out of it. Jesus got to the home, and everyone was so distraught. You can imagine the crying, weeping, and sorrow. Jesus looked at them and said, "Don't be upset. She's not dead; she's only asleep." Their sorrow turned to mocking, ridiculing, and making fun. "What do you mean she's not dead? Of course she's dead." What Jesus did next is very significant. It's a key to living in victory. It says they "mocked and jeered at Him, and Jesus put them out." Notice that the Son of God asked them to leave. He showed them the door. Jesus knew the importance of having people around Him who understood His destiny. His attitude was: *I don't need your doubt. I don't need you telling Me what I can't do. I'm going to surround Myself with believers, with people of faith, with people who understand My assignment.*

If you have people close to you who are constantly pulling you down, telling you what you can't do and how you'll never accomplish your dreams, understand that it is scriptural to show them the door. It may be difficult, but you have to have the attitude: *I cannot fulfill my destiny with your critical spirit in my life. I can't become who I was created to be with your negative spirit dragging me down. I love you, but I can't allow you in my inner circle. I'm going to love you from a distance.*

This is what Jesus did. He only took the little girl's parents and Peter, James, and John into the girl's room. He spoke to that girl, and she came back to life. Think of this. Jesus could have healed her in front of the whole laughing, mocking, ridiculing crowd. He's God, and He can do anything. But He was showing us this principle: Who you have in your inner circle is extremely important. If Jesus went to the trouble to ask the wrong people to leave, if He took the time to weed out the doubters, the naysayers, and the people who didn't believe in Him, if He was that concerned about His inner circle, how much more concerned should we be with who's in our inner circle?

Pay attention to who's on your team. Who's speaking into your life? To whom are you giving your time and attention? In practical terms, who are you eating lunch with every day at the office? Who are you talking to on the phone so much? Are they building you up or tearing you down? Are they pushing you toward your destiny, or are they telling you what you can't do? Are they modeling excellence, integrity, character, and godliness, or are they lazy, sloppy, and undisciplined? You have a responsibility to redeem your time.

Don't waste it with people who don't sharpen you. If you don't politely show them the door, that can keep you from your destiny. Sometimes we know a person's not good for us, we know they're dragging us down, but we think if we let them go, we're going to be lonely. Yes, you may be lonely for a season, but you'll never give up something for God without Him giving you something better back in return. God will not only give you new friends, He'll give you better friends. People who inspire you, people who celebrate you, and people who push you forward.

This may mean that you have to change who you eat lunch with at the office every day. That person who's always finding fault, critical, and badmouthing the boss; you don't need that poison in your life. That's not redeeming the time. You may have to change hanging out with that neighbor who's always depressed, defeated, and has a sad song. If you stay there, you're going to end up defeated. It's better to make the change and be lonely for a season than to be poisoned for a lifetime.

Don't Waste Another Day

When we come to the end of our days, God is going to ask us, "What did you do with the time I entrusted to you? Did you develop your gifts and talents? Did you accomplish your assignment?

How did you spend your life?" It's not going to be a good excuse to say, "God, I know I got distracted, but my friend got me off course." "God, I lived bitter, but somebody did me wrong." "God, I was negative, but my company let me go." I'm asking you to quit making excuses and start redeeming the time. We're not always going to be here. The Scripture says, "Our life is like a mist. We're here for a moment, then we're gone."

Make this decision that you're going to be an on-purpose person. Set your goals and be disciplined to stick with it. Don't waste any more days. Prune those relationships that are not adding to your life. And don't go to bed with any kind of defeat, bitterness, or negativity still in your mind. This day is a gift. Make sure you're investing your time and not wasting it. If you do this, the seeds of greatness inside you are going to take root and begin to flourish. You're going to see God's favor in new ways.

5

Stay Passionate

Studies show that enthusiastic people get better breaks. They're promoted more often, have higher incomes, and live happier lives. That's not a coincidence. The word *enthusiasm* comes from the Greek word *entheos*. *Theos* is a term for "God." When you're enthusiastic, you are full of God. When you get up in the morning excited about life, recognizing that each day is a gift, you are motivated to pursue your goals. You will have a favor and blessing that will cause you to succeed.

People of excellence stay passionate throughout their lives. Too many people have lost their enthusiasm. At one time they were excited about their futures and passionate about their dreams, but along the way they hit some setbacks. They didn't get the promotions they wanted, maybe a relationship didn't work out, or they had health issues. Something took the wind out of their sails. They're just going through the motions of life; getting up, going to work, and coming home.

God didn't breathe His life into us so we would drag through the day. He didn't create us in His image, crown us with His favor, and equip us with His power so that we would have no enthusiasm. You may have had some setbacks. The wind may have been taken out of your sails, but this is a new day. God is breathing new life into you. If you shake off the blahs and get your passion back, the winds will start blowing once again—not against you, but for you. When you get in agreement with God, He will cause things to shift in your favor.

On January 15, 2009, Captain Chesley "Sully" Sullenberger successfully landed a massive passenger airplane in the Hudson River after the plane's engines were disabled by multiple bird strikes. Despite the dangers of the jet plane landing in icy waters, all 155 passengers and crew members survived. It's known as the "Miracle on the Hudson." Just after the successful emergency landing and rescue, a reporter asked a middle-aged male passenger what he thought about surviving that frightening event. Although he was shaken up, cold and wet, the passenger had a glow on his face and an excitement in his voice when he replied, "I was alive before, but now I'm *really* alive." After facing a life-and-death situation, the survivor found that his perspective had changed. He recognized each moment as a gift and decided that instead of just living, he would start *really* living.

Seeds of Greatness

My question is, Are you *really* alive? Are you passionate about your life or are you stuck in a rut, letting the pressures of life weigh you down or taking for granted what you have? You weren't created to simply exist, to endure, or to go through the motions; you were created to be *really* alive. You have seeds of greatness inside. There's something more for you to accomplish. The day you quit being excited about your future is the day you quit living. When you quit being passionate about your future, you go from living to merely existing.

In the natural, there may not be anything for you to be excited about. When you look into the future, all you see is more of the same. You have to be strong and say, "I refuse to drag through this day with no passion. I am grateful that I'm alive. I'm grateful that I can breathe without pain. I'm grateful that I can hear my children playing. I am grateful that I was not hurt in that accident. I'm grateful that I have opportunity. I'm not just alive—I'm *really* alive."

This is what the apostle Paul told Timothy: "Stir up the gift, fan the flame." When you stir up the passion, your faith will allow God to do amazing things. If you want to remain passionate, you cannot let what once was a miracle become ordinary. When you started that new job you were so excited. You told all your friends. You knew it was God's favor. Don't lose the excitement just because you've had it for five years.

When you fell in love after meeting the person of your dreams, you were on cloud nine. You knew this match was the result of God's goodness. Don't take it for granted. Remember what God has done.

When your children were born, you cried for joy. Their births were miracles. You were so excited. Now you have teenagers and you're saying, "God, why did You do this to me?" Don't let what was once a miracle become so common that it's ordinary. Every time you see your children you should say, "Thank You, Lord, for the gift You've given me."

We worked for three years to acquire the former Houston Rockets basketball arena for our church. During that time, it was still being used for sports and music events. When there wasn't a ball game or concert, Victoria and I would go there late at night and walk around it. We'd pray and ask God for His favor. When the city leaders approved our purchase in 2001, we celebrated. It was a dream come true. Over twenty years later, it's easy to get used to. Holding services in such a huge building could become common, ordinary, and routine because we've been doing it so long now. But I have to admit that every time I walk in the building, I can't help but say, "God, thank You. You have done more than I can ask or think."

Live in Amazement

We all have seen God's goodness in some way. God opened a door, gave you a promotion, protected you on the freeway, and caused you to meet someone who has been a blessing. It was His hand of favor. Don't let it become ordinary. We should live in amazement at what God has done. When I look at my children, I think, *God, You're amazing*. When I see Victoria, I think, *God, You've been good to me*. Driving up to my house, I think, *Lord, thank You for Your favor*.

Don't let your miracles become so common that they don't excite you anymore. I read about a famous surgeon who continued to go to work every day even into his late eighties. He loved medicine. His staff tried to get him to retire and take it easy, but he wouldn't do it. He had invented a certain surgical procedure that he had performed over ten thousand times. It seemed so routine and so ordinary. He'd done it again and again. The surgeon was asked if he ever grew tired of performing his procedure. He said, "No, because I act like every operation is my very first one." He was saying, "I don't take for granted what God has allowed me to do. I don't let it become so ordinary that I lose the awe."

What has God done for you? Do you have healthy children? Do you have people to love? Do you have a place to work? Do you realize your gifts and talents come from God? Do you recognize what seemed like a lucky break was God directing your steps? There are miracles all around us. Don't take them for granted. Don't lose the amazement of God's works. Fan your flames. Stir up your gifts.

Sometimes we hold back, thinking we'll get excited when the next best thing comes along. Only then will we allow that spring back in our step. But I've learned if you aren't happy where you are, you won't get where you want to be. You need to sow a seed. Maybe nothing exciting is going on; perhaps you're facing big challenges. You could easily grow discouraged and give up on your dreams. But you are sowing a seed when you go to work with a smile, give it your best, offer kindness to others, and show gratitude for what you have. God will take that seed and grow it to bring something exciting into your life. The Scripture tells us God will take us from glory to glory and from victory to victory. You may be in between victories right now, but keep your passion and hold on to your enthusiasm. The good news is, another victory is on its way, and so is another level of glory and another level of God's favor.

Put Your Heart into It

Ecclesiastes says, "Whatever you do, do it with all your heart and you are honoring God." When you give 100 percent effort, you do it to the best of your ability; because you're honoring God, you will have His blessing. That means it will go better. It will be easier and you will accomplish more.

Let's make it practical. When you do the dishes, don't complain; do it with all your heart and you honor God. When you mow the lawn, don't drag around all sour. Mow it with enthusiasm. Mow it like you're on a mission from God. With every step, thank God that your legs work. Thank God that you're healthy. At the office, don't give it a half-hearted effort. Don't just do what is required to get by. You're not working unto people. You're working unto God. Do it with all your heart. Do it with a smile. Give it your very best.

When I was growing up, there was a police officer who directed traffic at the Galleria Mall in Houston. His assignment was to keep people safe on one of the busiest intersections in the city. Traffic could be backed up for five or ten minutes. He didn't just direct traffic like normal, he practically danced while he directed. Both hands would be constantly moving. He had a whistle and he held his head like a drum major. His feet would dance here and there. He could direct traffic and moonwalk at the same time. He really put on a show. Drivers pulled over just to watch him. He did not drag through the day. He didn't feel bad about going to work. He was passionate.

That's the way you should be. Don't drag through the day. Don't get stuck in a rut. Whatever you do, put your heart into it. Put a spring in your step. Wear a smile on your face. You honor God when you do it with all your heart. That's being a person of excellence.

Be the Best That You Can Be

The Scripture says God has given us the power to enjoy what's appointed and allotted to us, which means I don't have the power to enjoy your life. You may have more money, more gifts, more friends, and a better job. But if you put me in your life, I will not enjoy it. You are uniquely created to run your own race. Quit wishing you were someone else or thinking, *If I had his talent*... If God wanted you to have his talent, He would give it to you. Take what you have and develop it. Make the most of your gifts. Instead of thinking, *If I had her looks*..., be grateful for the looks God gave you. That's not an accident. The life you have is perfectly matched for you.

Why don't you get excited about your life? Be excited about your looks, your talent, and your personality. When you are passionate about who you are, you bring honor to God. That's when

God will breathe in your direction and the seeds of greatness He's planted inside will spring forth.

Really, it's an insult to God to wish you were someone else. You are saying, "God, why did You make me subpar? Why did You make me less than others?" God didn't make anyone inferior. He didn't create anyone to be second class. You are a masterpiece. You are fully loaded and totally equipped for the race that's designed for you. Your attitude should be: *I may not be as tall, as tan, or as talented as someone else, but that's okay. Nobody will ever be a better me. I'm anointed to be me. I'm equipped to be me. And not only that, it's also easy to be me.*

It's easy to be yourself. It's easy to run your race because you're equipped for what you need. But so many times people try to be something they are not. I've known dark-skinned people who apply cream to try to be lighter. And I know light-skinned people who go to a tanning bed to try to be darker. I had an older lady touch my hair at a book signing once. She said, "Joel, I wish I had that curly hair." Nowadays you can do something about it. If you have straight hair and you want curly hair, you can perm it. If you have gray hair and you want brown hair, dye it. If you have no hair and you want hair, buy it!

Keep Working and Growing

If you want to stay passionate, you have to stay productive. You have to have a reason to get out of bed in the morning. When you're not producing, you're not growing. You may retire from your job, but don't ever retire from life. Stay busy. Keep using your mind. Keep helping others. Find some way to stay productive. Volunteer at the hospital. Babysit your relatives' children. Mentor a young person.

When you quit being productive, you start slowly dying. God promises if you keep Him first place, He will give you a long, satisfied life. How long is a long life? Until you are satisfied. If you quit producing at fifty and you're satisfied, the promise is fulfilled. I don't know about you, but I have too much in me to die right now. I'm not satisfied. I have dreams that have yet to be realized. I have messages that I've yet to give. I have children to enjoy, a wife to raise...I mean a wife to enjoy. I have grandchildren yet to be born. When I get to be about ninety, and I'm still strong, still healthy, still full of joy, and still good-looking, then I'll say, "Okay, God, I'm satisfied. I'm ready for my change of address. Let's go."

Some people are too easily satisfied. They quit living at fifty. We don't bury them until they are eighty. Even though they've been alive, they haven't been really living. Maybe they went through disappointments. They had some failures or somebody did them wrong and they lost their joy. They just settled and stopped enjoying life. But God has another victory in your future. You wouldn't be breathing if God didn't have something great in front of you. You need to get back your passion. God is not finished with you.

God will complete what He started in your life. The Scripture says God will bring us to a flourishing finish—not a fizzling finish. You need to do your part and shake off the self-pity, shake off what didn't work out. You may have a reason to feel sorry for yourself, but you don't have a right. God said He will take what was meant for your harm and not only bring you out, but also bring you out better off than you were before.

Get in Agreement with God

In the Scripture, David said, "Lift up your head and the King of glory will come in." As long as your head is down and you are discouraged, with no joy, no passion, and no zeal, the King of glory will not come. Instead, get up in the morning and say, "Father, thank You for another day. Thank You for another sunrise. I'm excited about this day." When you're really alive, hopeful, grateful, passionate, and productive, the King of glory, the Most High God, will come in. He'll make a way where it looks like there is no way.

We all face difficulties. We have unfair things happen. Don't let it sour your life. Just because you had a bad break doesn't mean your life is over. I know a popular minister who led his church for many years and was such a great speaker that he was in constant demand. But several years ago, he was diagnosed with Parkinson's disease. He eventually lost the ability to speak and had to resign from his church. He once was so eloquent, strong, and vibrant, but it looked as if his career was over. It looked as if his best days were behind him. But just when things started to look really bad for him, he sent me a manuscript with a note: "Joel, as you know, I can't speak anymore, so I've taken up writing. Here's a look at my newest book."

Just because you can't do what you used to do doesn't mean you're supposed to sit on the sidelines. If you can't speak, write. If you can't run, walk. If you can't stand up, just sit up. If you can't dance, shake your head. If you can't sing, tap your foot. Do whatever you can do. As long as you have breath, you have something in you. Don't lose your passion.

Think about the apostle Paul. He was thrown in prison unfairly at the peak of his career. Just when it was all coming together, he had this major disappointment. Paul could have become depressed and thought, *Too bad for me*. He could have given up on his dreams. Instead, he kept his passion. While in prison, he wrote four books of the New Testament. What looked like a setback was really a setup for God to do something greater in Paul's life.

You may have been through some bad breaks and unfair situations. Stay passionate. God is still on the throne. If you keep your head up, the King of glory will still come in and guide you to where He wants you to be.

Look Ahead

It's tempting to go through life looking in the rearview mirror. When you are always looking back, you become focused on what didn't work out, on who hurt you, and on the mistakes you've made. "If only I would have finished college." "If only I'd spent more time with my children." "If only I'd been raised in a better environment." As long as you're living in regret, focused on the negative things of the past, you won't move ahead to the bright future God has in store. You need to let go of what didn't work out. Let go of your hurts and pains. Let go of your mistakes and failures. You can't do anything about the past, but you can do something about right now. Whether it happened twenty minutes ago or twenty years ago, let go of the hurts and failures and move forward. If you keep bringing the negative baggage from yesterday into today, your future will be poisoned.

You can't change what's happened to you. You may have had an unfair past, but you don't have to have an unfair future. You may have had a rough start, but it's not how you start, it's how you finish. Don't let a hurtful relationship sour your life. Don't let a bad break, a betrayal, a divorce, or a bad childhood cause you to settle for less in life. Move forward and God will pay you back. Move forward and God will vindicate you. Move forward and you'll come into a new beginning. Nothing that's happened to you is a surprise to God. The loss of a loved one didn't catch God off guard. God's plan for your life did not end just because your business didn't make it, or a relationship failed, or you had a difficult child.

My question is, Will you become stuck and bitter, fall into self-pity, blame others, and let the past poison your future? Or will you shake it off and move forward, knowing your best days are still ahead?

The next time you are in your car, notice that there's a big windshield in the front and a very small rearview mirror. The reason the front windshield is so big and the rearview mirror is so small is that what's happened in the past is not nearly as important as what is in your future. Where you're going is a lot more important than where you've been.

Ditch the Baggage

If you stay focused on the past, you'll get stuck where you are. That's the reason some people don't have any joy. They've lost their enthusiasm. They're dragging around baggage from the past. Someone offended them last week, and they've got that stuffed in their resentment bags. They lost their tempers or said some things they shouldn't have. Now, they've put those mistakes in their bags of guilt and condemnation. Ten years ago, their loved one died and they still don't understand why; their hurt and pain is packed in their disappointment bag. Growing up, they weren't treated right. There's another suitcase full of bitterness. They've got their regret bags, containing all the things they wish they'd done differently. Maybe there is another bag with their divorce in it, and they are still mad at their former spouse, so they've been carrying resentment around for years. If they tried to take an airline flight, they couldn't afford it. They've got twenty-seven bags to drag around with them everywhere they go.

Life is too short for you to live that way. Learn to travel light. Every morning when you get up, forgive those who hurt you. Forgive your spouse for what was said. Forgive your boss for being rude. Forgive yourself for mistakes you've made. At the start of the day, let go of the setbacks and the disappointments from yesterday. Start every morning afresh and anew. God did not create you to carry around all that baggage. You may have been holding on to it for years. It's not going to change until you do something about it. Put your foot down and say, "That's it. I'm not living in regrets. I'm not staying focused on my disappointments. I'm not dwelling on relationships that didn't work out, or on those who hurt me, or how unfairly I was treated. I'm letting go of the past and moving forward with my life."

You should focus on what you can change, not what you cannot change. What's done is done. If somebody offended you, mistreated you, or disappointed you, the hurts can't be undone. You can get bitter, pack it in a bag, carry it around, and let it weigh you down, or you can forgive those who hurt you and go on. If you lost your temper yesterday, you can beat yourself up and put the guilt and condemnation in a bag, or you can ask for forgiveness, receive God's mercy, and do better today. If you didn't get a promotion you wanted, you can get sour and go around with a chip on your shoulder, or you can shake it off, knowing that God has something better in store. No matter what happens, big or small, if you make the choice to let it go and move forward, you won't let the past poison your future.

I know a woman who went through a divorce years ago. We prayed several times in our services, asking God to bring a good man into her life. One day she met a fine godly man who was very successful. She was so happy, but she made the mistake of carrying all her negative baggage from her divorce into the new relationship. She was constantly talking about what she had been through and how she was mistreated. She had a victim mentality. The man told me later that she was so focused on her past and what she had been through that he just couldn't deal with it. He moved on. That's what happens when we hold on to the hurts and pains of the past. It will poison you wherever you go. You can't drag around all the personal baggage from yesterday and expect to have good relationships. You have to let it go.

Quit looking at the little rearview mirror and start looking out the great big windshield in front of you. You may have had some bad breaks, but that didn't stop God's plan for your life. He still has amazing things in your future. When one door closes, stay in faith and God will open another door. If a dream dies, don't sit around in self-pity talking about what you lost. Move forward and dream another dream. Your life is not over because you lost a loved one, went through a divorce, lost a job, or didn't get the house you wanted. You would not be alive unless God has another victory in front of you.

Get Ready for the New Things God Has in Store

I heard a story about a forty-year-old lady having open-heart surgery. She had blockage in one of her arteries and had to have bypass surgery. Although this is a delicate procedure, it's considered a routine surgery and performed successfully more than 200,000 times every year.

During the operation, the surgeon clamped off the main vein flowing to the heart and hooked it to a machine that pumps the blood and keeps the lungs working. The heart actually stops beating while the vein is being bypassed. When the procedure is over and the machine is removed, the warmth from the body's blood normally causes the heart to wake back up and start beating again. If that doesn't work, they use drugs to wake up the heart.

This lady was on the operating table and the

bypass was finished, so they let her blood start flowing, but for some reason her heart didn't start beating. They gave her the usual drugs with no success. She had no heartbeat. The surgeon massaged her heart with his hand to stimulate that muscle and get it beating again, but even that did not work. The surgeon was so frustrated, so troubled. It looked as if she was finished. After doing everything he could medically, he leaned over and whispered in her ear, "Mary, I've done everything I can do. Now I need you to tell your heart to beat again." He stepped back and heard *bump, bump, bump*. Her heart kicked in and started beating.

Do you need to tell your heart to beat again? Maybe you've been through disappointments and life didn't turn out as you hoped. Now you're just sitting on the sideline. You have to get your passion back. Get your fire back. Tell your heart to dream again. Tell your heart to love again. Tell your heart to laugh again. Tell your heart to believe again.

Give Life All You've Got

I have a friend who went through a divorce after twenty-six years of marriage. His wife left him a note saying she had found someone else. He had been an outgoing, fun, and energetic person. But after his wife left him, he was solemn, discouraged, and had no joy, no life. I told him what I'm telling you: "This is not the end. God has a new beginning. But you have to do your part and tell your heart to beat again." Little by little, he recovered his joy, his vision, and his passion. Then God brought a beautiful lady into his life and they married. He told me that he's happier than he's ever been.

You may have suffered a setback, too, but don't sit around in self-pity. Tell your heart to beat again. Tell your heart to love again. Someone may have done you wrong, but don't let it poison you. Tell your heart to forgive again. Maybe a dream didn't work out, but nothing will change if you just expect more of the same. Tell your heart to dream again. You may have let the pressures of life weigh you down, and you're all solemn and serious. You need to tell your heart to laugh again. Tell your heart to smile again. Get back your joy. Get back your enthusiasm.

Jesus says in the book of Revelation, "I have one thing against you, you have left your first love." The Scripture doesn't say you've lost love; it says you've left your first love. That means you can go get it. You haven't lost your passion. You just left it. Go get it. You haven't lost the love for your family; you've just left it. Now go get it. You haven't lost that dream. It's still there in you. You just left it. You have to go get it.

Stir up what God put inside. Fan the flame. Don't be just barely alive. God wants you to be really alive. You may have had some setbacks, but this is a new day. Dreams are coming back to life. Your vision is being renewed. Your passion is being restored. Hearts are beating again. Get ready for God's goodness. Get ready for God's favor.

You *can* live a life of victory. You *can* overcome every obstacle. You *can* accomplish your dreams. You *can* set new levels for your family. Not only are you able, but I also declare you *will* become all God created you to be. You *will* rise to new levels. You *will* live a blessed, successful, rewarding life. My encouragement is: Don't settle where you are.

You have seeds of greatness inside. Put these principles into action each day. Get up in the morning expecting good things, then go through the day positive, focused on your vision, running your race, knowing that you are well able. Excellence is in your DNA. The Most High God breathed His life into you. You have what it takes. This is your time. This is your moment. Shake off doubts, shake off fear and insecurity, and get ready for favor, get ready for increase, get ready for the fullness of your destiny.

About the Author

JOEL OSTEEN is a *New York Times* bestselling author and the senior pastor of Lakewood Church in Houston, Texas. Millions connect daily with his inspirational messages through television, podcasts, Joel Osteen Radio on Sirius XM, and global digital platforms.

We Want to Hear from You!

Each week, I close our international television broadcast by giving the audience an opportunity to make Jesus the Lord of their lives. I'd like to extend that same opportunity to you. Are you at peace with God? A void exists in every person's heart that only God can fill. I'm not talking about joining a church or finding religion. I'm talking about finding life and peace and happiness. Would you pray with me today? Just say, "Lord Jesus, I repent of my sins. I ask You to come into my heart. I make You my Lord and Savior."

Friend, if you prayed that simple prayer, I believe you have been "born again." I encourage you to attend a good Bible-based church and keep God first place in your life. For free information on how you can grow stronger in your spiritual life, please feel free to contact us.

Victoria and I love you, and we'll be praying for you. We're believing for God's best for you, that you will see your dreams come to pass. We'd love to hear from you!

To contact us, write to:

Joel and Victoria Osteen
PO Box #4271
Houston, TX 77210

Or you can reach us online at JoelOsteen.com.